For Rocky. *H.W.*

First published in Great Britain 2023 by Red Shed,
part of Farshore

An imprint of HarperCollins*Publishers*
1 London Bridge Street
London SE1 9GF
www.farshore.co.uk

HarperCollins*Publishers*
Macken House, 39/40 Mayor Street Upper, Dublin 1
D01 C9W8

Text and illustrations copyright © HarperCollins*Publishers* 2023
ISBN 978 0 0085 2440 1
Printed in the UK by Bell and Bain Ltd, Glasgow.
001

Consultancy by Dr Miquela Walsh, DEdPsych, MsC (Dist),
BSc (Hons), HCPC accredited.

A CIP catalogue record for this book is available from the British Library.

Hannah Wilson

Samara Hardy

WORRIES BIG AND SMALL WHEN YOU ARE 7

RED SHED

What if . . .

What if I worry about stuff?

A worry is an uncomfortable feeling about a situation.
It might be a feeling of fear about a strange noise or a feeling
of nervousness about a trip to the hospital. EVERYBODY worries
about stuff. Big stuff, little stuff, all kinds of stuff. You might
think some of your worries are silly. They're NOT. All worries
are important as they can stop us from doing things.

Worries are a normal part of life. We can't get rid of all of them,
but we can stop them bossing us around. The best way to deal
with a worry is to TALK ABOUT IT with a grown-up you trust.
In this book, I call this person 'your grown-up'. Your grown-up
is probably your mum, dad or the person who looks after you
– or all three! You can tell your grown-up (or grown-ups)
ANYTHING. It can be hard talking about things that worry
us, but it's lovely to get a hug and a thank you for being so
brave for sharing our feelings. So let's get chatting about
tricky stuff and stop worries getting in the way of fun!

WORRIES BOTHER US AT DIFFERENT AGES.
IF YOU ARE OLDER OR YOUNGER THAN SEVEN,
THIS BOOK IS STILL FOR YOU!

What if a bee is buzzing around?

The bee won't bother you if you don't bother the bee. So don't try to catch or touch the little fellow. Watch quietly as it goes about its buzzy business. What IS that buzzing sound? It's made by the insect's four wings moving very quickly.

Where's the bee going? If it lands on a flower, watch it suck up NECTAR (sweet liquid) with its straw-like mouthpart. Can you see yellow powder sticking to the bee's leg or bristly body? That's POLLEN. It will fertilize the next flower the bee lands on, making seeds for new flowers!

Some bees make honey!

THERE WILL BE PLENTY OF OTHER PARTIES AND PLAYDATES!

What if I don't get invited to a party?

This happens to ALL of us from time to time. Missing out usually makes ME feel a little jealous. Jealousy is NORMAL. It's wishing we could do something another person is doing or have something they have. Have YOU ever felt like that? How does missing out on a party or playdate make you feel?

It might help to chat about these feelings with your grown-up. It DOESN'T help to wonder WHY you weren't invited. You'll never know for sure, but it's probably not because someone doesn't like you. Try to cheer yourself up. What do you find fun or relaxing.

What if I hate having my hair cut?

Grab your grown-up and write a list of the things that bother you about hair cuts. Make a plan to deal with each thing, one by one. If you find having a hair cut BORING, you could plan to take a book. If you worry about SCISSORS, remind yourself that hairdressers are trained experts who know how to use them safely.

Now make a list of the fun things at the hairdresser's. (Yes, I did say FUN.) The magically rising chair, the bubbly hair wash, those flowing wizardy gowns! What POSITIVE (good) things can YOU come up with?

What if the food at school is all weird?

The school is not a fancy restaurant and you won't be able to eat your favourite food for every meal. So even if school lunch tastes like an old sock dipped in mud, try to shovel it down so that it can give your body energy. As your body grows and changes, your TASTE will change too. So keep munching lots of different foods and one day that muddy-sock lunch might taste SUPER YUMMY!

What if I hear a strange noise?

Let me guess. You're on your own, sitting on the sofa, looking at a book. Suddenly, there's a RATTLE, CREAK or BANG! Terrified, you dive behind the sofa and start shaking like a very cold leaf! Am I right? Has this ever happened to YOU? It must be hard to DIVE behind a sofa, so perhaps I got that bit wrong. But you know what I mean: SCARY NOISES! What can we do about them? Any ideas?

How about starting with a DEEP BREATH. Then if your imagination starts inventing moaning monsters or bellowing baddies, tell it to STICK TO THE FACTS. Buildings are noisy. Windows rattle in the wind, washing machines rumble, and water pipes creak as they get bigger when hot or shrink when cold. Beyond your own walls, cars vroom, neighbours drop saucepans and cats wail.

So make like a detective and use that clever brain of yours to try to work out what REALLY made those sounds. Interview your grown-up if you need help uncovering the facts. Good job, detective!

What if I'm shorter than my friends?

Every classroom is full of children of different heights. Children grow at different speeds at different ages, and being smaller than your friends does NOT mean you are not growing properly. Is it being DIFFERENT that bothers you?

We don't look exactly the same as each other. We are bigger or smaller, darker or paler, with curlier or straighter hair. Are these differences IMPORTANT? Are tall people always clever? Does brown hair make someone nice? Do blue eyes mean they're grumpy?

It's normal to compare ourselves to others, but it's as helpful as a chocolate teapot. If you can, forget your height and other OUTSIDE bits and concentrate on your INSIDE bits. It's your amazing MIND that will help you have fun, do cool stuff and be the wonderful person you are.

What if the skateboard ramp is too fast and high?

Sometimes it's good to FACE OUR FEARS so they don't stop us missing out on things that could be fun – like a ramp, slide, rope bridge or zip wire. Do this slowly with SMALL STEPS. Step 1 could be standing at the top of the ramp and just having a look. Step 2 could be your grown-up holding you as you roll down. What about Step 3? Any ideas? YOU (not me) are in charge of your small steps. Fingers crossed, soon you'll be in charge of that pesky fear too. Just TALKING about fears shows how brave you are. Great job!

SAY NO TO ANYTHING THAT MAKES YOU FEEL UNCOMFORTABLE.

What if my grown-up leaves without me?

That would NEVER happen. If they needed to go somewhere, they'd tell you that another trusted person would look after you. Do you have other questions about keeping safe in the park? BEFORE you next go out, chat about what to do in different situations. What should you do if you couldn't find your grown-up? Meet by the skateboard ramp or STAY WHERE YOU ARE and wait for your grown-up to find you?

What if a stranger asks me to go off with them?

Don't go. Never walk off with anyone who isn't your grown-up. Shout, "NO!" loudly and run to your grown-up. Tell them what happened. You can tell your grown-up ANYTHING. Even bad, embarrassing and weird stuff, or when you think you've done something wrong. You can even tell your grown-up secrets that someone might have told you not to tell. You can ALWAYS tell. Your grown-up will make everything OK and you will not get into trouble. You'll get a big hug for telling and talking.

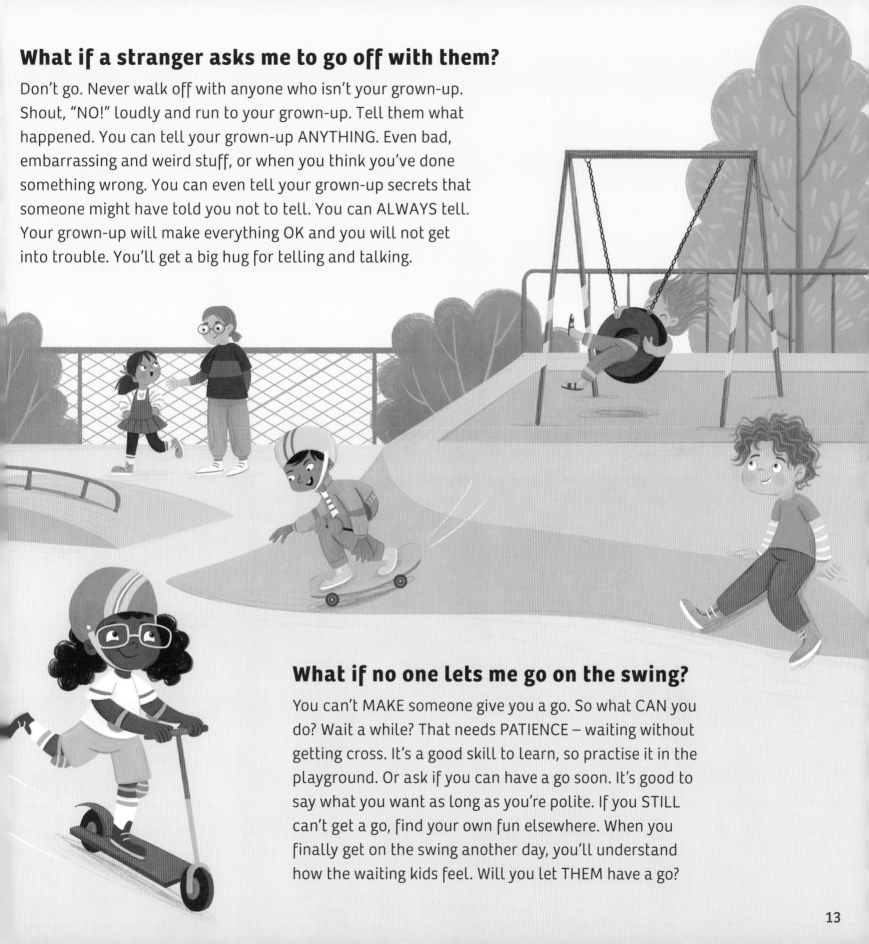

What if no one lets me go on the swing?

You can't MAKE someone give you a go. So what CAN you do? Wait a while? That needs PATIENCE – waiting without getting cross. It's a good skill to learn, so practise it in the playground. Or ask if you can have a go soon. It's good to say what you want as long as you're polite. If you STILL can't get a go, find your own fun elsewhere. When you finally get on the swing another day, you'll understand how the waiting kids feel. Will you let THEM have a go?

What if I have to go to hospital?

Our normal doctor can help us with most illnesses, aches and pains. But sometimes, they might suggest we visit the hospital. A hospital is bigger, with more equipment and more people to help us get better. The doctors and nurses in a hospital are SPECIALISTS – experts in particular things, such as ears, tummies or bones.

Most people have been to hospital – ask your grown-up for THEIR hospital stories. The doctors and nurses see children just like you often, but it's OK to feel nervous. We can get nervous about things that haven't happened yet or things we don't understand. So ask your grown-up to try to explain what might happen during the visit. You could write questions for the doctors and nurses.

HOSPITALS HAVE MEDICINE TO STOP PAIN.

Many hospital visits are just like going to see your normal doctor. First, you'll sit in the waiting room – BORING! So bring a book and a snack. Then you'll see the doctor for a chat. You might need a special treatment, such as an X-ray, an eye test or some surgery. Surgery is usually when medicine sends you to sleep so that the doctors can treat your body.

If you need to stay overnight, GOOD NEWS: Hospitals have beds, bathrooms, kitchens and often playrooms with toys and a telly! Your grown-up would sleep on a small bed next to you. YOU get the special big bed. What would you pack? Don't forget teddy!

When you leave hospital, you'll understand more about your amazing body. And you'll have your very own hospital story to tell.

Imagine worries rising from your head, floating up into the clouds and blowing away.

What if my friend says I've got to marry someone in my class?

You don't. When people get married, their love is different from friendship love or family love. When you're a grown-up, you might want to marry someone or you might not. Right NOW, you don't need to think about any of that romantic stuff.

You also don't need to do whatever your friends say, especially if it doesn't feel right for YOU. What could you say to your friend? Have a think. How about: "No, I don't. I can make my OWN decisions about what I do."

WORDS CAN HURT TOO. WHAT CAN YOU DO IF SOMEONE SAYS SOMETHING MEAN?

What if someone hits me?

WALK AWAY and find your grown-up or a teacher. Tell them if your body hurts. Like any rough behaviour, hitting can be shocking. It can make us feel sudden strong emotions such as fear or anger. Often it makes us cry. How does rough behaviour make YOU feel? It's good to have a chat with someone while these emotions fade. Hopefully, whoever hit you will say sorry, but try not to think about them too much. Look after YOURSELF.

What if I need a poo at school?

Let me guess. The school loos are stinky, the doors don't shut properly and the toilet paper feels as rough as a hedgehog's bum. And there isn't enough TIME to go. Anything else? Tell your grown-up because when we SHARE our worries, we can work out how to WAVE THEM GOODBYE.

When I was little, I had to walk down a long creepy corridor to get to the school toilets. I told my mum and she asked the teaching assistant to take me in future. THANKS, MUM!

School may not be the perfect place to poop. I'm sure you'd rather be at home where it's quieter and the toilet paper is less hedgehoggy. But it's good to LISTEN TO YOUR BODY. When it yells, "WEE NOW!" or "POOP PLEASE!", take it to the loo. You'll feel much more comfortable.

's OK to make
tinky smells
d funny noises
n public loos.
at's just how
r bodies work!

Tell your teacher if you need help or more toilet time.

What if my grown-up kisses me goodbye and it's so embarrassing?

EMBARRASSMENT – worrying about what people think of us – is a common feeling. But we can't REALLY know what others think, so should we waste time wondering? Your classmates probably don't notice your grown-up kissing you. They're too busy feeling embarrassed by THEIR grown-up singing loudly or blowing their nose like a walrus!

If YOU think something is fine, try to do it. The more you do it, the less you might feel embarrassed. But if you feel VERY uncomfortable about anything, make a plan with your grown-up. If those kisses cause too many worries, could you try a hug instead or a goodbye kiss around the corner?

What if I don't want to learn my spellings for the test?

If you DID practise the spellings, would you do better in the test? How would that feel? Sometimes we need to put in EFFORT to get good feelings. You need to decide whether it's worth it or not. Is it worth walking up a hill to get a good view? Is it worth baking for an hour to get a dreamy creamy cake? Is it worth looking at your spellings for 20 minutes to do better in the test? Think how PROUD of your effort you'll feel. It might be best to just get the job done!

What if I make a mistake in front of the whole class?

When we make a mistake, it means we are trying something tricky that we haven't mastered yet. We're learning. But making mistakes in front of other people is tough. What worries YOU about it? Sometimes it makes ME worry that people will think I'm stupid. Do you ever feel like that?

But when you see someone get something wrong, do you think THEY are stupid? No, me neither. I think they are BRAVE for trying. Can YOU be brave? Can you put up your hand and answer a question? Give it a go. The more you do it, the easier it will get. Try tricky things and make some marvellous mistakes!

18

We all make mistakes.
Mistakes help us learn.

Smart kids ask for help!

What if my teacher is mean?

I am sorry you are finding your teacher difficult. Can you tell your grown-up about the times you feel the teacher was mean? Together, chat about whether the teacher was being FAIR. If you were juggling the school's pet rabbits, and your teacher told you off, were they being mean or fair?

Even if they WERE being fair, it's not nice when a grown-up is cross. But it doesn't mean the teacher doesn't like you. They just didn't like your ACTIONS. You are in control of your actions – so next time, no rabbit-juggling!

But perhaps you think the teacher was NOT being fair? My old teacher once thought I had ripped a page from a book. I hadn't. When I got told off, I felt angry and nervous in my tummy. Just like my teacher, YOUR teacher is not perfect. They will make mistakes. And sometimes, they might be tired and grumpy. That's unfair for you, but hopefully your teacher won't be like that for long. Let the tricky time pass. What could cheer you up?

What if I have to perform in assembly?

How are you feeling? Nervous? That's normal. But GOOD NEWS: Scientists say nervousness can help us concentrate and give us energy. It can make us perform better! Perhaps you're worried about making a mistake? That might happen. No performance is perfect. Just KEEP GOING and your audience probably won't even notice. Alongside the nerves and mistakes, I think you'll also find some FUN as you strum that air guitar, read that poem or sing that song. What a great achievement to perform in public, you SUPERSTAR!

What if my friend tells me something, but I'm not sure it's true?

When someone says there's a dragon in the wardrobe, it's handy to know if that's TRUE or not – so we can call a fire engine before it sets fire to our pants!

But HOW can we judge whether something is true or false? Think clearly and sensibly. You probably know dragons don't exist in real life, so there CAN'T be one in your wardrobe. Make up your OWN mind and trust your feelings. If you have a sneaky feeling your buddy is showing off with a made-up scary story, then maybe they are. Sometimes you just have to ignore the silly things people say!

What if we miss our bus stop?

There are many situations grown-ups handle so you don't have to, such as travelling on a bus or train. Your grown-up knows when to get off – unless they have fallen asleep. WAKE UP!

On the bus, there's usually a bell to let the driver know you want the next stop. Could you ring it when the right time comes? Even if you DO miss the stop, NO PROBLEM. When Plan A doesn't work out, activate Plan B! What could Plan B be? Discuss with your grown-up whether you could get on another bus or walk a little bit further.

THERE'S ALWAYS A PLAN B!

What if it's sports day and I have butterflies?

What are those butterflies telling you? Is the nervous fluttery feeling in your tummy because you're EXCITED? You want to zoom past all your buddies and win every race! Or are you NERVOUS because you really don't fancy running around in front of lots of people. Perhaps you're worried you will fall over or come last in everything?

LISTEN CAREFULLY TO INSTRUCTIONS. BEING PREPARED WILL HELP YOU RELAX AND PERFORM BETTER.

There are different reasons for butterflies because we are all different. Some of us find sport and P.E. easy and exciting, while others are champions of singing, coding or writing stories. But ALL of us can find some fun on sports day. So put on your trainers, grab your water bottle and get ready for action with my TWO TOP TIPS:

1. DON'T COMPARE YOURSELF TO OTHERS. "But it's a competition!" I hear you holler. "It's all about comparing how fast we run, how far we throw, and who comes first or last!" You're right. But you can't control how the other kids do, so focus on doing YOUR best. Then, even if you come last, you are still working on yourself, improving, getting fit and being an all-round champ.

HELPING OTHERS GIVES US A BREAK FROM WORRYING ABOUT OURSELVES.

2. BE A GOOD TEAM PLAYER. If your classmates fall over, help them up. If they can't find the start line, show them. Comfort them when they don't win and high-five them when they do. Even if they beat you. If you show everyone what a fantastic team player you are, good feelings will bounce around and EVERYONE will have a great day.

Are you feeling more ready now? I hope so. On your marks, get set, GO!

What if I'm worried about climate change?

Climate change is the warming of Earth and the changing of its weather patterns. It is caused by humans, such as when power stations burn coal to make electricity. This releases gases that wrap around our planet, trapping in HEAT. As Earth warms, our natural areas change, making it hard for some people and animals to live safely.

Many grown-ups are working hard to save the planet, developing 'green' ways to make electricity. Let THEM worry. Instead, can you do something USEFUL? How about turning off lights when you leave a room? That saves electricity, so less coal is burnt.

What if I accidentally drop a glass and it smashes?

Keep still. If you walk about or try to tidy up, you might cut yourself. So call for a grown-up. You won't get into trouble – EVERYONE breaks things from time to time. The grown-up will be impressed by your honesty and awareness of safety.

Do you know WHY the accident happened? Were you on tippy toes trying to grab the glass from a high shelf? Or were you trying to read a book, drink water and hop on one leg all at the same time? If so, you know how to avoid an accident next time!

REAL LIFE IS MORE BORING AND MUCH SAFER THAN FILMS!

SHARING A FEAR BY TALKING ABOUT IT CAN MAKE IT SMALLER.

NEW MONSTER MOVIE!

What if I can't stop thinking about the scary baddie in the film?

Often the more we try NOT to think about scary or worrying things, the more they tumble around inside our head. So I suggest we DO try to think about this baddie. Let's FACE THE FEAR. First, can you tell your grown-up WHY the silly-billy baddie is so scary?

When I face my fears about a film baddie, I research how it was invented. Was the monster drawn on a computer or is it a big squidgy costume? If the baddie is a person, what's the actor's real name? The FACTS help me sweep away fears about the scary FICTION. Do you have your own ideas about how to face fears?

What if I'm worried my grown-up is going to die?

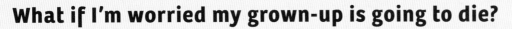

Death is a very sad but natural stage of our life cycle. Most people die when they are very old, much older than your grown-up. When someone dies, it means we can never see them again. So just THINKING about our loved ones dying makes us feel sad, even if it hasn't happened yet.

When we worry about someone, it shows that we are caring people, full of LOVE. But when our worries bother us, it can help to talk about them. So have a hug with your grown-up and try to tell them about any sad thoughts. You can ask them questions about death and dying too.

None of us know what will happen in the future, good or bad. When you think about the future, the things that haven't happened yet, can you think of some GOOD things? What happy stuff might the future hold?

What if a babysitter is coming?

It's normal to feel a little WOBBLY when your grown-up goes out and someone else looks after you. Are YOU feeling wobbly? Let's think about WHY. Will you miss your grown-up and worry about them? I do understand. But they'll be just fine, and back before you know it. Ask them to give you a kiss when they get home – even if you're asleep!

Are you worried the babysitter won't know what to do? Could you show them the important stuff? Teddies, books, biscuits? They won't do everything EXACTLY the way your grown-up does, but new things can be FUN. Your babysitter might like to build chip towers! Your grown-up will love hearing about this, and will be SO grateful you helped them have a night out.

What if there's a flood?

Get some information. Ask your grown-up if you live in an area that could flood. Floods can happen after very heavy rain makes rivers overflow. Most areas do NOT experience them.

Ask about OTHER natural events too. You'll probably discover that wildfires, earthquakes and hurricanes don't take place where you live either. But even if they DO, science is on your side. Scientists can usually predict when these events will happen so that the grown-ups can prepare. You would have plenty of time to leave the area until it was safe to return again.

What if I've got no one to play with?

What is worrying you about this? Being lonely or bored? We all have to get used to being on our own every now and then. ALONE TIME is great for relaxing quietly with a book or doing things our pals don't usually want to do, such as making a drumkit with pots and pans. What could you do for YOUR alone time?

On a busy beach or in the playground, ask one of the kids if you can play with them. If they say no, have some fun on your own. Your amazing IMAGINATION can invent a game just for you!

What if my grown-up tells me off, but I didn't do anything wrong?

I wonder WHY your grown-up told you off? Did they make a mistake? Did they tell you off for purple handprints on the wall, but the prints weren't yours? This mistake IS unfair for you. But everyone makes mistakes, even your grown-up.

Just tell the truth as best you can. You can't make your grown-up believe you, but you can feel good inside if you know you behaved well. If you don't understand WHY your grown-up told you off, ask them to explain. Perhaps you can learn if you need to act differently next time.

What if I don't want to go to bed?

Let's think about WHY you're not jumping for joy when your grown-up yells, "Bedtime!" Are you TOO BUSY to go to bed or is your room TOO DARK? Perhaps you don't want to be on your own or you just can't be bothered to brush your teeth? Or are you an OWL? I can't guess why and neither can your grown-up. So talk to them and cook up ideas to ease each worry.

As the worries get smaller, try to make the bedtime GOOD STUFF bigger. Think about how important it is to rest your body and mind. Think about teddies, snuggly duvets, cuddles and books that send you on dreamy adventures. Is your bed a better place to be now? I hope so. Unless you really ARE an owl, of course!